# SIDESPLITTING
## JOKES
## FOR
# MINECRAFTERS

## GHASTLY GOLEMS AND
## GHOULISH GHASTS

**BRIAN BOONE**

Illustrations by Amanda Brack

Sky Pony Press
New York

Copyright © 2017 by Hollan Publishing, Inc.

Minecraft ® is a registered trademark of Notch Development AB

The Minecraft game is copyright © Mojang AB

Sky Pony Press books may be purchased in bulk at special discounts for sales promotion, corporate gifts, fund-raising, or educational purposes. Special editions can also be created to specifications. For details, contact the Special Sales Department, Sky Pony Press, 307 West 36th Street, 11th Floor, New York, NY 10018 or info@skyhorsepublishing.com.

Sky Pony® is a registered trademark of Skyhorse Publishing, Inc.®, a Delaware corporation.

Minecraft ® is a registered trademark of Notch Development AB
The Minecraft game is copyright © Mojang AB

Visit our website at www.skyponypress.com.

10 9 8 7 6 5 4 3 2

Library of Congress Cataloging-in-Publication Data is available on file.

Cover design by Brian Peterson
Cover illustration credit Hollan Publishing, Inc.
Cover and interior illustrations by Amanda Brack

Print ISBN: 978-1-5107-1883-8
Ebook ISBN: 978-1-5107-1884-5

Printed in Canada

# CONTENTS

# INTRODUCTION

You're a major Minecraft player, so you know what it's like to dig, poke around, and search until you find the tools and treasures you're after. Well, congratulations: You just did that in real life—thanks for picking up *Jokes for Minecrafters: Ghastly Golems and Ghoulish Ghasts.*

It's unlike any other joke book you'll find in a store, library, school—well, pretty much anywhere in your "Overworld." That's because this book is all Minecraft jokes, all the time, with a special focus on those pesky mobs. Look out for ghasts, golems, witches, zombie pigmen, and all those other hostiles! No mods required to enjoy these hilarious jokes. And after all, it's time all those bad guys got taken down a peg. (Or should we say . . . a Notch.)

So the next time you need a break from Minecraft, dig into *Ghastly Golems and Ghoulish Ghasts.* We guarantee you'll have a "blast"—*ore* maybe a few!

# CHAPTER 1
## GOBS AND GOBS OF MOBS

**Q: How do skeletons organize their scare missions?**
A: They call each other on the tele-bone.

■

**Q: How do hostile mobs communicate?**
A: With mob-ile phones.

■

**Q: What do skeletons play in the Minecraft band?**
A: The trom-bone.

**Q: Did you hear about the murder of the snow golem?**
A: It's a cold case.

■

**Q: What did the skeleton say to the hostile wolf?**
A: Bone appetite!

■

**Q: How can you tell if a hostile mob is avoiding you?**
A: You keep calling them and they don't respawn.

**Q: What states would hostile mobs love to visit?**
A: North and South Scarolina.

■

**Q: You're trapped in a room with nothing but creepers, zombies, and skeletons. What gets killed first?**
A: You, because you can't kill all of them!

■

**Q: What kind of ore can kill a hostile mob?**
A: Die-monds.

**Q: What do snow golems eat?**
A: Ice scream.

**Q: How do snow golems travel?**
A: They ride an icicle.

■

**Q: What's a squid's favorite meal?**
A: Fish and ships.

**Q: Why should you never pick a fight with a squid?**
A: Because they're well-armed.

■

**Q: What do you call a snow golem in the desert?**
A: A puddle.

■

**Q: Why shouldn't you have a private conversation in a spider cave?**
A: Because the place is bugged.

■

**Q: Why do silverfish make terrible hockey goalies?**
A: They shy away from the net.

**Q: Why do silverfish save all their money?**
A: So they can one day be goldfish.

■

**Q: Why do cave spiders live in caves?**
A: Because if they lived in houses they'd be house spiders.

■

**Q: What's a squid's favorite kind of sandwich?**
A: A sub.

■

**Q: Why did the squid attack a ship in the morning?**
A: It wanted Captain Crunch for breakfast.

**Q: Where do cave spiders go for medical advice?**
A: Web MD.

■

**Q: Why did the cave spider spin a web?**
A: It didn't know how to knit one.

■

**Q: Are skeletons good learners?**
A: Sure. They keep an open mind.

■

**Q: How does a skeleton feel in the cold?**
A: Chilled to the bone.

**Q: Why do cave spiders live in caves?**
A: Because those are their cave-orite.

■

**Q: What does a skeleton shoot when it's dead?**
A: Marrows.

■

**Q: What do you get when you cross a spider and Steve?**
A: Game over!

■

**Q: Why are skeletons afraid of dogs?**
A: They don't want to get wolfed down.

**Q: What do you call a funny ocelot?**
A: A-mew-sing.

■

**Q: What do you call the rabbits that swarm you when you're holding a carrot on a stick?**
A: A hare-icane.

■

**Q: What's happening when a killer bunny attacks?**
A: A bad hare day.

■

**Q: What do you call sneaking up on a killer bunny?**
A: A hare-brained idea.

Q: **When a killer bunny wants you to do something, what do you do?**
A: You hop to it.

■

Q: **What's being chased by a killer bunny like?**
A: It's a hare-owing experience.

■

Q: **How do squids in Minecraft make each other laugh?**
A: With ten-tickles.

■

Q: **What do you get if you cross mushrooms with cave spiders?**
A: Terrible spaghetti sauce.

**Q: What are the heaviest creatures in Minecraft?**
A: Skele-tons.

■

**Q: How do you know Minecraft spiders are bored?**
A: They're climbing up the walls.

■

**Q: How do you make a skeleton laugh?**
A: You tickle its funny bone.

■

**Q: How does a spider stay in shape?**
A: It takes a spin class.

Q: **What do you call a Minecraft skeleton that won't bother to shoot arrows at Steve?**

A: A lazy bones.

■

Q: **Why are spiders so skittish?**

A: Because they're hanging on by a thread.

■

Q: **What food would skeletons love to get their hands on?**

A: Spare ribs.

■

Q: **What part of physics do spiders study?**

A: String theory.

**Q: What's a snow golem's favorite game?**
A: Freeze tag.

■

**Q: What do snow golems do on the computer?**
A: They surf the Winternet.

■

**Q: What's big and white and lives in the desert biome?**
A: A lost snow golem.

■

**Q: Where did the skeleton shoot the kid?**
A: In the kid-knees.

Q: **What do you call a nervous spider?**
A: A jitterbug.

■

Q: **Why did Alex flee?**
A: Because the spider spied her.

■

Q: **When are the spiders getting married?**
A: They want a big June webbing.

■

Q: **Why do spiders eat corn?**
A: So they can make cobwebs.

**Q: How was the spider driving in the mud?**
A: Spinning its wheels.

■

**Q: What's a skeleton's favorite TV show?**
A: *Bones*.

■

**Q: Why did the squid cross the ocean?**
A: To get to the other tide.

■

**Q: Why didn't Steve think the skeleton would attack him?**
A: Because it was gutless.

**Q: Why can Minecraft spiders spin?**
A: They have webbed feet.

**Q: How do doctors give skeletons their medicine?**
A: With knee-dles.

**Q: Why did the Minecraft player see a psychiatrist?**
A: To deal with the skeletons in his closet.

**Q: What do you call a wolf you find in the forest?**
A: A timber wolf.

**Q: What did Steve say to Herobrine?**

A: Nothing. Herobrine doesn't exist.

■

**Q: What's the difference between Steve and an archaeologist?**

A: Archaeologists actually like it when they find skeletons underground.

■

**Q: Why should you never tell pigs your Minecraft tricks?**

A: They always squeal.

■

**Q: Why do Minecraft horses eat with their mouths open?**

A: They have terrible stable manners.

Q: What are spider webs good for?
A: Spiders.

■

Q: What do you call an imaginary glass of saltwater that can save the day?
A: Herobrine.

■

Q: Why doesn't Minecraft have any bugs?
A: Because the spiders are there to eat them.

■

Q: What kind of underwear do spiders wear?
A: Spider jockeys.

**Q: What's a skeleton that goes out in the sun?**
A: A bone-head.

■

**Q: What do you get when skeletons walk into the sun?**
A: A bone-fire.

■

**Q: What happens when skeletons attack cows?**
A: Udder chaos.

■

**Q: Why are spiders so charming?**
A: They've got the world on a string.

**Q: What's the fastest fish in Minecraft?**
A: The one that got away.

■

**Q: Why did Alex give her rabbit a bath?**
A: Because her hare was dirty.

■

**Q: What do chickens do instead of mine?**
A: They eggs-cavate.

■

**Q: Why won't birds jump off cliffs in Minecraft?**
A: Because they're chicken.

**Q: What do you call a rabbit with stacks of diamonds and gold?**

A: A million-hare.

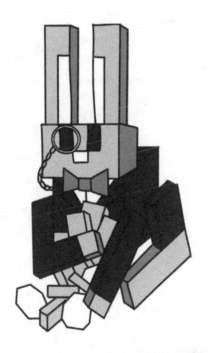

**Q: What happened when one snow golem got mad at the other snow golem?**

A: He gave him the cold shoulder.

Q: **What do snow golems wear on their heads?**
A: Ice caps.

■

Q: **Where do snow golems dance?**
A: At the snowball.

■

Q: **What do you call a snow golem with sharp teeth?**
A: Frostbite.

■

Q: **Why are skeletons so calm?**
A: Because nothing gets under their skin.

**Q: What do you call a lost dog in Minecraft?**
A: A where-wolf.

■

**Q: What happened when the wolf ate a clock?**
A: He got ticks.

■

**Q: What's black and white and red all over?**
A: A panda with a magma cube.

■

**Q: What's black and white and red all over?**
A: A sheep standing on obsidian looking for redstone dust.

**Q: Why are ocelots bad at hiding?**

A: Because they're always spotted.

**Q: What do you call a cow that's afraid of villagers?**

A: A Cow-ard.

■

**Q: What hats do skeletons hate?**

A: Knee caps.

**Q: What do snow golems eat for breakfast?**
A: Frosted Flakes.

■

**Q: What do you call an educated skeleton?**
A: A school-eton.

■

**Q: What old novel do squids and hostiles both love?**
A: *Mob-y Dick.*

■

**Q: Why did Steve teleport to a pig?**
A: He cast his pearls before swine.

**Q: What do skeletons eat?**
A: Bone meal.

■

**Q: Why did Steve punch an elephant?**
A: He saw the trunk and thought it was a tree.

■

**Q: What superhero lives in a Minecraft cave, man?**
A: Spider, Man.

■

**Q: How can you tell if an elephant is in your house?**
A: He's stuck in the doorway.

**Q: How are Steve and an elephant similar?**

A: They both think a trunk is pretty important.

■

**Q: Why are ocelots the only big cats in Minecraft?**

A: Do you really want a game full of cheetahs?

■

**Q: Did you hear about the time every hostile showed up at the same time?**

A: It was mob-scene!

■

**Q: Why are hostile mobs like playing cards?**

A: They come in a pack.

Q: **What day should you watch out for spiders?**
A: Websday.

■

Q: **What's as sharp as a skeleton's arrow?**
A: His next arrow.

■

Q: **How many spiders does it take to screw in a light bulb?**
A: None. They prefer the darkness.

■

Q: **How do you obtain a pincushion in Minecraft?**
A: Run through a mob of skeletons.

**Q: Why do sheep in Minecraft try to run away?**
A: They're baaaaashful.

■

**Q: What do you call two squids that look alike?**
A: I-tentacle twins.

■

**Q: How do hostiles get money?**
A: They mob a bank.

■

**Q: Why did the sheep keep falling down the mineshaft?**
A: Because it couldn't make a ewe-turn.

Q: **What's the difference between a diamond and a bunch of rabbit food?**

A: One is 14 karats, and one is 14 carrots.

■

Q: **What do you call a skeleton dance party?**

A: A grave rave.

■

Q: **What do you call a spider dance party?**

A: A cave rave.

■

Q: **What do you get if you cross a squid with a minecart?**

A: A crustacean wagon

■

Q: **How did Steve avoid getting shot by a skeleton?**

A: He had an arrow escape.

# CHAPTER 2
## ZOMBIE ATTACK!

**Q: Why can you always find a zombie pigman at the farmer's market?**

A: They prefer flesh ingredients.

■

**Q: What do you call a zombie pigman that steals your sword?**

A: A HAMburglar.

■

**Q: Why couldn't the zombie pigman escape the pit of lava?**

A: He was too much of a slow-pork.

Q: **Why did the zombie want to go on a date with Alex?**
A: She had braaaaaaaaains.

■

Q: **What's black and white and dead all over?**
A: A zombie in a tuxedo.

■

Q: **What time do zombies show up in Minecraft?**
A: At ate o'clock.

■

Q: **What do a butcher shop and a cave full of zombies have in common?**
A: They're both full of dead meat.

**Q: Why aren't zombie pigmen appreciative?**
A: They take things for grunted.

■

**Q: Why did the zombie pigman cross the road?**
A: He was riding a chicken.

■

**Q: What did the zombie say to the Enderman?**
A: "Copycat!"

■

**Q: What do zombies and these jokes have in common?**
A: They're brainless.

**Q: What's a zombie's favorite game?**
A: *Mindlesscraft.*

■

**Q: What's a zombie's best quality?**
A: Dead-ication.

■

**Q: What did the zombie say to Steve?**
A: Nice gnawing you!

Q: **What do you get if you cross a pig with a zombie?**
A: Cooked pork chops.

Q: **What were the creeper and the zombie arguing about?**
A: At first it sounded like something about snakes and there was a lot of groaning, but it then it all ended with a bang.

Q: **Did you hear about the big zombie party?**
A: Yeah, it was pretty dead. Full of stiffs.

**Q: What do you call a zombie with lots of kids?**

A: A mom-ster.

**Q: Did you know it's really easy to kill zombies in Minecraft?**

A: Yep, it's a real no-brainer.

**Q:** Where should you never go in Minecraft if you're avoiding Zombies?

A: Dead ends.

■

**Q:** What would you get if you crossed a zombie with a snow golem?

A: Frostbite.

■

**Q:** What does an upset zombie do?

A: It falls to pieces.

■

**Q:** What kind of weather does a zombie like?

A: When it raaaaaaains.

**Q: Where does a zombie sit?**

A: On his zombie-hind.

■

**Q: Why did the zombie cross the road?**

A: To eat the chicken.

**Q: Under what kind of stone would you find a zombie?**
A: A tombstone.

■

**Q: What should you do if you're surrounded by zombies?**
A: That you're only playing Minecraft, and that it's not real life.

■

**Q: What kind of karate can you use on zombie pigmen?**
A: Pork chops.

■

**Q: Why are zombie pigmen the dullest creatures in Minecraft?**
A: They're all such boars.

Q: **Why don't zombies like jokes?**
A: They've got a rotten sense of humor.

■

Q: **What's a zombie's favorite band?**
A: The Grateful Dead.

■

Q: **What do you get when you cross a zombie and a chicken?**
A: A rotten egg.

**Q: Why do zombies run around so much in the morning?**
A: Because they get all fired up.

■

**Q: What does a zombie who spawns right before dawn have?**
A: Rotten luck.

■

**Q: What do you call a zombie with a bell?**
A: A dead ringer.

**Q: Why did the zombie and skeleton exercise in the morning?**

A: To feel the burn!

**Q: Why was the zombie hard to interrogate?**

A: He was harder to break than obsidian.

**Q: What day is a zombie most likely to attack?**
A: Chews-day.

■

**Q: What do zombies think of Minecraft?**
A: They a-door-it.

■

**Q: When do zombies do most of their shopping?**
A: During door-buster sales.

■

**Q: Why are zombies bad at hide-and-seek?**
A: You can always hear them groaning.

**Q: When do zombies sleep in Minecraft?**
A: When they're dead tired.

■

**Q: What's a zombie's favorite holiday?**
A: Day of the Dead.

■

**Q: What kind of buildings would zombie pigmen construct?**
A: A sty-scraper.

■

**Q: What kind of machine can move a zombie pigman?**
A: A pork-lift.

**Q: What's a zombie's favorite food?**
A: Blood oranges.

■

**Q: Where did all those zombies get hired for Minecraft?**
A: Monster.com

■

**Q: What do you call a zombie with three eyes?**
A: A Zombiiie.

■

**Q: What happened when a zombie attacked a cow?**
A: Zombeef.

Q: **What do you do if a mob of 100 zombies surrounds your house?**
A: Hope that it's Halloween!

Q: **Do zombies eat dinner with their fingers?**
A: No, they eat the fingers separately.

Q: **Do zombies smell as bad as they look?**
A: Only a phew.

**Q: What do you get if you try to grab a zombie pigman?**
A: Pulled pork.

■

**Q: Who's the smartest zombie pigman?**
A: Albert Einswine.

■

**Q: What's the best part about being killed by zombies in Minecraft?**
A: At least there's pretty music playing in the background!

Q: **What do you call a zombie with no eyes?**
A: A zombe.

■

Q: **What card game do zombie pigmen play?**
A: Porker.

Q: **What do you call a skeleton riding a chicken, and a
baby zombie riding a spider?**
A: Opposite Day.

**Q: Why does zombie pigmen's skin look the way it does?**
A: Because of zombie pigment.

■

**Q: What did the door say to the zombie?**
A: "You crack me up!"

■

**Q: How do you know a zombie pigman was just there?**
A: They left a note and the oink was still dry.

■

**Q: Did you hear about the pig transforming into a zombie pigman?**
A: It was shocking!

# CHAPTER 3

## SWITCHING TO WITCHES

**Q: What's happening if you see a character with potions?**

A: Trouble is brewing.

**Q: What do you call a not very hostile mob of witch?**

A: Well, probably not a witch!

Q: What goes "*cackle, cackle, BOOM!*"
A: A witch in a mineshaft explosion.

■

Q: Where do witches play Minecraft?
A: On a HexBox.

■

Q: What do witches use to keep their skin so dry, gross, and scaly?
A: Potion lotion.

■

Q: Why should you give a name to every witch you come across in Minecraft?
A: So you can remember which witch is which.

Q: **What do you call a witch in possession of lots and lots of potions?**
A: Wrich!

■

Q: **What's worse than getting attacked by a witch?**
A: Getting attacked by two witches.

■

Q: **What do witches yell out before you destroy them?**
A: "Bow no!"

■

Q: **What's the number-one illness affecting witches?**
A: Potion sickness.

**Q: Why can't miners understand witches?**

A: They're from a completely different regeneration.

■

**Q: How do you get a witch to kick the bucket?**

A: Throw the bucket at her!

■

**Q: How can you tell if a witch spawned inside your house?**

A: She's calling you and demanding broom service.

■

**Q: How is meeting a witch in Minecraft like going to a swimming pool?**

A: You're going to get splashed!

Q: **What's the difference between a versatile baseball player and a sword?**

A: One is a switch-hitter, and one is a witch-hitter.

■

Q: **How long will you feel tired after a witch throws a potion at you?**

A: All weak.

■

Q: **When is a witch pretty?**

A: When she's a pretty scary witch.

■

Q: **How can you tell if a witch made your pizza?**

A: It has way more spider eyes on it than usual.

**Q: What do you call a not very hostile witch?**
A: Anything but a witch.

■

**Q: What goes "*cackle, cackle, BOOM!*"**
A: A witch in a mineshaft explosion.

■

**Q: Why can't witches go near schools?**
A: Because they were ex-spelled.

■

**Q: What do witches use to keep their skin dry and scaly?**
A: Potion lotion.

Q: **What's another name for a mob of witches?**
A: Broom-mates.

■

Q: **Did you hear about the dog trainer who joined a hostile mob?**
A: She went from wags to witches.

■

Q: **Why did the witches stop hunting Steve to play croquet?**
A: They were wicket witches.

■

Q: **What do witches drink for energy?**
A: Apple spider.

**Q: How do witches get good deals when they go shopping?**

A: They love to hag-gle.

■

**Q: Why did the witch like her own potions?**

A: They brew her away!

■

**Q: What do you call a recently spawned witch?**

A: A baby broomer.

■

**Q: How do you get a witch to back off?**

A: Tell her she looks be-witching.

Q: **Where do witches go on vacation?**
A: Witch-ita, Kansas.

Q: **What do you get if you cross a witch and a snow golem?**
A: A cold spell.

Q: **What do you get if you cross a witch and a blaze?**
A: A hot spell.

Q: **How do witches send packages?**
A: FedHex.

**Q: What do you call a wealthy witch?**
A: Richie witch.

■

**Q: What state is full of witches?**
A: Hexas.

■

**Q: What do you call pants for witches?**
A: Witches' britches.

■

**Q: What game do witches play?**
A: *Witchcraft.*

**Q: How good was the witch's brew?**
A: It was hex-tra special.

■

**Q: Where do witches go when they're sick?**
A: The witch doctor.

■

**Q: How do witches get places?**
A: They witch-hike.

■

**Q: What happened when Steve faked an attack on a witch?**
A: The witch twitched.

**Q: How do witches get instantly to the sea?**
A: An ocean potion.

■

**Q: What do witches love about computers?**
A: Spell check.

■

**Q: How do you greet witches in Minecraft?**
A: "Hello, Hello, Hello!"

■

**Q: How do witches tell time?**
A: With a witch watch.

Q: **How do you make a witch leave you alone?**
A: You make her scratch.

■

Q: **How do you make a witch scratch?**
A: Take away the W.

■

Q: **Where do witches like to brew their potions?**
A: In their coven's ovens.

■

Q: **What's the difference between a lever and a member of a hostile mob bearing potions?**
A: One is a switch and the other is a witch!

# CHAPTER 4

## IS THIS "THE END?" NETHER YOU MIND ABOUT THAT

**Q:** Did you hear about the miner who died in the Nether?

**A:** Yeah, he fell head over heels in lava.

■

**Q:** What happens if you cross a female horse with the Nether?

**A:** A night-mare.

■

**Q:** What European country loves Minecraft the most?

**A:** The Nether-lands.

**Q: Why is Belgium filled with lava?**
A: It's next to the Nether-lands.

■

**Q: Why's it so hard to grow crops in the Nether?**
A: They always Wither.

■

**Q: What happened when the blaze got a job?**
A: He got fired.

■

**Q: What kind of crackers should you serve a Blaze?**
A: Firecrackers.

**Q: What do you call the first person who discovered blazes?**
A: Crispy.

■

**Q: What does the enter sign say at a store in the Nether?**
A: Enter, man.

■

**Q: What are Nether parties known for?**
A: Being ghast-ly.

■

**Q: What happened when Steve got killed in the Nether?**
A: He vowed to nether return.

Q: Why are Enderman like the sun?
A: They're impossible to look at.

■

Q: Why are Steve's pets always being eaten in the Nether?
A: Ghasts love hot dogs.

■

Q: What happened to Steve when he went through the final portal?
A: He reached The End.

■

Q: How do you stay warm in the Nether?
A: Put on a Nether jacket.

**Q: How do you make an Enderman leave you alone?**
A: Throw water on him!

■

**Q: What city would an Enderman most like to visit?**
A: Teleportland.

■

**Q: What's on the back of a cart in the Nether?**
A: An ender fender.

■

**Q: What eats wood in Minecraft?**
A: Endermites.

Q: Pretend you're in Minecraft and an Enderman is chasing you. What do you do?

A: Stop pretending!

■

Q: What did the Enderman do when he saw Steve with a diamond?

A: He took the diamond and ran away!

■

Q: What did the Enderman wear to the dance?

A: Black.

■

Q: What's the difference between an Enderman and a magician?

A: Nobody minds when a magician disappears and reappears.

**Q: How does an Enderman get to the top of a tall building?**

A: He takes the stares.

■

**Q: Why did the Enderman say "knock-knock"?**

A: Because it was stuck in the wrong joke.

■

**Q: What do you call an ender dragon who boasts about all the miners it's destroyed?**

A: A braggin' dragon.

■

**Q: What do you call an ender dragon falling from the sky because it's tired?**

A: A saggin' dragon

**Q: How do you stop an ender dragon from charging?**
A: Take away its credit cards.

■

**Q: What would you find in an ender oyster?**
A: Ender pearls.

■

**Q: Why did the ender dragon burn down his house?**
A: He liked home cooking.

■

**Q: Why does the Enderman keep getting recruited for the military?**
A: Because they think he's army material.

**Q: What game do minecrafters play when they're not playing Minecraft?**

A: *Dungeons and Ender Dragons.*

■

**Q: What kind of bugs do Endermen spawn?**

A: Ender dragonflies.

■

**Q: Where should you put ender treasure?**

A: Ender chest.

■

**Q: Why did the waterpark in the Nether shut down?**

A: Because no water blocks were allowed.

Q: **What should you call the loot found down in the spooky Nether?**

A: Loooooooooot!

Q: **What do chickens lay in the Nether?**

A: Hard boiled eggs.

Q: **What kind of party can you have in the Nether?**

A: A fire-ball!

Q: **What grew on Steve's face after too much time in the Nether?**

A: Netherwarts.

**Q: What happened when Steve encountered Wither?**
A: It was heart-breaking.

**Q: What did Steve say when he found the stronghold?**
A: "This is a-mazing."

**Q: What do you call the first miner who discovered a blaze?**
A: Toast.

**Q: What's a blaze's favorite day of the week?**
A: Fry-day.

Q: **What happened when Santa Claus met a blaze?**
A: He turned into Crisp Kringle.

■

Q: **What's black and white and red all over?**
A: A wither skeleton, a skeleton, and some redstone.

■

Q: **What did Steve say when the Wither skeleton tried to attack him?**
A: "Let's sword this thing out!"

■

Q: **What the difference between Minecraft and fairy tales?**
A: When you reach The End of a fairytale, it's a happy ending.

# CHAPTER 5

## CREEPERS? JEEPERS!

**Q: What did the polite creeper say when he bumped into someone?**

A: "Sssssssssssssscuse me."

■

**Q: Who's a creeper's closest relative?**

A: His sssssssssisssssster.

■

**Q: How do creepers listen to music?**

A: On a boombox.

**Q: What's a creeper's favorite TV show?**
A: *The Big Bang Theory.*

■

**Q: What's the difference between a creeper and a balloon?**
A: One blows itself up and the other you have to blow up yourself.

■

**Q: How do creepers see?**
A: With creepers' peepers.

■

**Q: What goes "*crack, crack, whoosh, pop, hisssss*?"**
A: A creeper chewing bubble gum.

**Q: Who's a creeper's favorite detective?**
A: Ssssssssssssherlock Holmes.

■

**Q: What was the creeper's favorite subject in school?**
A: Hisssssssstory.

■

**Q: What time is it if you see almost a dozen ocelots chasing after a creeper?**
A: Ten after one.

■

**Q: What's green and has four wheels?**
A: A creeper. We were kidding about the wheels.

Q: **What do you get when you mix a creeper with a cow?**
A: Exploding milk!

■

Q: **What did the ocelot cause for the creeper?**
A: A cat-astrophe.

■

Q: **What's the difference between a creeper and a dirt block?**
A: Both explode. Except for the dirt block.

■

Q: **Where do creepers keep their stuff?**
A: In their creep-purse.

**Q: Who's a creeper's favorite actress?**
A: Meryl Creep.

■

**Q: What can kill you even though it's unarmed?**
A: Creepers.

■

**Q: Why wasn't the creeper invited to the party?**
A: Because it had an explosive personality.

■

**Q: What kind of car does a creeper drive?**
A: A creep Jeep.

Q: How does a creeper take his drinks?
A: With iccccccccce.

■

Q: What should you sleep with if creepers are nearby?
A: One eye open.

■

Q: What was Steve doing near a mob spawner?
A: Creeping warm.

■

Q: What's scarier than a giant horde of creepers?
A: Not much!

**Q: What's black and white and green all over?**

A: A creeper on a malfunctioning screen.

◼

**Q: Why did Steve throw eggs at creepers?**

A: He wanted them ssscrambled.

◼

**Q: What kind of music do creepers listen to?**

A: Pop music.

◼

**Q: Does a house get scared when creepers are near?**

A: Sure. The windows get shudders!

Q: **What's green, explodes, and wears a hat?**
A: A creeper in a hat.

■

Q: **Why did the creeper cross the road?**
A: To blow up the people on the other side.

■

Q: **Why didn't the creeper cross the road?**
A: There was an ocelot on the other side.

■

Q: **Why do creepers drop discs when they're shot by skeletons?**
A: It's their way of saying "For the *record,* you didn't kill me."

**Q: If you crossed a creeper with a tree, what would grow on it?**

A: Mosssssssss.

■

**Q: What's a creeper's favorite thing to do on a playground?**

A: The ssssssssslide.

■

**Q: What's a creeper's second-favorite thing to do on a playground?**

A: Sssssssswings.

■

**Q: What do you get when you cross a creeper and a cow?**

A: Steak.

Q: **What you get when you cross a creeper with a comedian?**

A: I don't know, but it's hissssssterical.

■

Q: **What do creepers do after they argue?**

A: They hiss and make up.

■

Q: **What says sssiiiih sssiiiih?**

A: A backwards creeper.

■

Q: **What happens on February 29th in Minecraft?**

A: Creep Day.

**Q: What's scary, ugly, and deep green?**
A: A creeper holding its breath.

■

**Q: Why didn't the creeper get pinched on St. Patrick's Day?**
A: Because it was green from head to toe (and also because
   nobody is going to pinch a creeper).

■

**Q: What's a creeper's favorite kind of book?**
A: Myssssssteries.

■

**Q: How do you address a creeper's father?**
A: Missssssssster.

**Q: What does a creeper do when it doesn't get its way?**
A: It throws a hisssssssy fit.

■

**Q: What did the creeper instructor say to its students?**
A: "Pay attention. I'm only going to do this once."

■

**Q: Where does a creeper keep their homework?**
A: In a trapper creeper.

■

**Q: What do you call a napping hostile?**
A: A creeper sleeper.

**Q: What's a good name for a creeper?**
A: Sissy.

■

**Q: What kind of cheese do creepers hate?**
A: Limburger.

■

**Q: What was the only kind of cheese left after a creeper blew up a house?**
A: De-Brie.

■

**Q: What's a dead creeper's favorite kind of music?**
A: Disc-go.

Q: **What do you call a creeper riding an elephant?**
A: Sir.

Q: **What hisses louder than a creeper?**
A: Two creepers.

Q: **Why was the creeper ill-equipped to join the army?**
A: Because it was unarmed.

**Q: What do you call two creeper spawns and a pigman?**
A: Green Eggs and Ham.

■

**Q: What's green with red spots?**
A: A creeper with the measles.

■

**Q: What do creepers hate to waste money on?**
A: Sleeves.

Q: **What did the skeleton get after it killed a creeper?**
A: A slipped disc.

Q: **Why are creepers green?**
A: So they can hide in lime gelatin!

Q: **How many creepers does it take to destroy hours of work and make you quit the game?**
A: Just one!

# CHAPTER 6

## SLIME TIME

**Q: What's green, lives in a swamp, and is slimy?**
A: Slime.

■

**Q: What kind of texture do slime have?**
A: A slimy one!

■

**Q: What did one slime say to the other slime?**
A: "Do you mind if I stick with you?"

**Q: Why don't zombies eat slime?**
A: They haven't got the brains.

■

**Q: Why was the slime turned away from the restaurant?**
A: It had a no shirt, no shoes, no service policy.

■

**Q: Why did Steve throw slime out the window?**
A: He wanted to see slime fly.

**Q: What kind of TV shows do slime watch?**
A: Slime dramas.

■

**Q: How do slime keep shoes on?**
A: They tie the laces in a snot.

■

**Q: What's green and hangs from a tree?**
A: Slime in a tree.

■

**Q: What would you call slime wearing a helmet?**
A: A snail.

Q: **How do you know you've met a slime?**
A: They stick with you all day.

■

Q: **What do your nose and the Nether have in common?**
A: Both are full of slime.

■

Q: **What's hostile and sticks to the roof of your mouth?**
A: A slime sandwich.

■

Q: **What do you get when you cross slime with peanut butter?**
A: Something that *really* sticks to the roof of your mouth.

**Q: What do you call a smaller slime?**
A: Slim.

■

**Q: What do you call it when a big slime jumps Steve?**
A: A sticky situation.

■

**Q: What's brown and sticky?**
A: Slime in a brown shirt.

■

**Q: How does a Nether mob close doors?**
A: It slimes them shut.

**Q: What did Steve say when the slime attacked?**
A: "Ooze going to save me?"

■

**Q: What's big, red, and eats slime?**
A: A big, red slime-eater!

■

**Q: What happens when slime goes into the water?**
A: It gets wet.

■

**Q: What's slime's favorite drink?**
A: Slimeade.

**Q: Why are slime annoying?**
A: Because when you're having fun, slime flies!

■

**Q: Why should you never tell a secret to slime?**
A: Because only slime will tell.

■

**Q: What did the big slime say to the little slime?**
A: "Stick with me and we'll go places!"

■

**Q: What do school lunch and Slime have in common?**
A: Everything!

**Q: How do you start a story in the swamp biome?**
A: "Once upon a slime…"

■

**Q: Why did the gross creature live in a swamp?**
A: It wanted to live in the slimelight.

■

**Q: What hostile is the most sluggish?**
A: Slime.

**Q: What does a little slime say?**
A: "Goo goo!"

**Q: What game is popular in the swamp biome?**
A: Slimon Says.

**Q: How do you compliment slime?**
A: Tell it it's doing a goo job.

Q: **What do a hopper block and a slime have in common?**

A: One is a hopper, and the other . . . is also a hopper!

■

Q: **What's the most untrustworthy slime?**

A: Sly-me.

■

Q: **What does the slime do when it needs to go?**

A: It hops to it.

**Q: What did the slime say to the creeper?**
A: "Father, is that you?"

■

**Q: What did Steve say after the slime left?**
A: "What a slimeball!"

■

**Q: What's the difference between a frog and slime?**
A: The frog eats flies, and that's about it.

Q: Why don't slime spawn in spots full of mushrooms?
A: Because mushrooms are slimy enough.

■

Q: Why couldn't the slime get around to spawning?
A: Because it was swamped.

■

Q: What is it if you see a red magma cube and a green slime together?
A: Christmas!

**Q: When did Steve find the dropped slimeballs?**
A: Just in slime!

**Q: What did the Minecrafter say to the slime block?**
A: "Let's bounce!"

Q: **What do you get when you cross slime with a boat?**
A: An ooze cruise.

■

Q: **What kind of praise do slime get?**
A: "Ooze" and "aaaahhhhs!"

# CHAPTER 7

## KNOCK-KNOCK.
## YOU SCARED?

Knock-knock.
Who's there?
A creeper.
A creeper who?
*BOOM!*

■

Knock-knock.
Who's there?
Mine.
Mine who?
Mine if I take your diamonds?

■

Knock-knock.
Who's there?
Nether.
Nether who?
You're Nether going to let me in, are you?

■

Knock-knock.
Who's there?
Wither.
Wither who?
I'm coming in Wither you want me to or not!

■

Knock-knock.
Who's there?
Lettuce.
Lettuce who?
Lettuce in, there are creepers out here!

■

Knock-knock.
Who's there?
Slime.
Slime who?
Slime to get out of the house.

■

Knock-knock.
Who's there?
Enderman.
Aaaaaaaaah!

■

Knock-knock.
Who's there?
Hostile mob.
Hostile mob who?
Does it matter?

■

Knock-knock.
Who's there?
Interrupting creeper.
Interrupting creeper wh—
Sssssssssss.

■

Knock knock…
Who's there?
Sssssssss…
Nobody's home!

■

Knock knock…
Who's there?
Endermite.
Endermite who?
Let me in, end-er-mite leave you alone!

■

Knock-knock.
Who's there?
Snow golem.
Ssssssnow golems here. Just us creepersssssss.

■

Knock-knock.
Who's there?
Boo.
Boo who?
Sorry, I didn't know a sad ghast lived here.

■

Knock-knock.
Who's there?
Ssmoo.
Ssmoo who?
Creeper pretending to be a cow.

■

Knock-knock.
Who's there?
Creeper.
Creeper who?
Creeper in your windows blowing your people up!

■

Knock-knock
Who's there?
Easily distracted zombie.
Easily distracted zomb—
Chicken!

Knock-knock.
Who's there?
I'm green . . .
I'm green who?
*Booooooooom!*

Knock-knock.
Who's there?
Zombie.
Zombie who?
The zombie who's going to break down your door!

Knock-knock.
Who's there?
Witch.
Witch who?
Would I what?

■

Knock-knock.
Who's there?
Nether.
Nether who?
Nether mind.

■

Knock-knock.
Who's there?
Not a.
Not a who?
Not a creeper!

■

Knock-knock.
Who's there?
Nether.
Nether who?
Nether ask me.

■

Knock-knock.
Who's there?
Wither.
Wither who?
Wither where?

■

Knock-knock.
Who's there?
Ender dragon.
Ender dragon who?
Ender dragon this joke out!

■

Knock-knock.
Who's there?
Jack o' lantern.
Jack o' lantern who?
Jack o' lantern before dark. The mobs are coming!

■

Knock-knock.
Who's there?
Quit button.
Quit button who?
Quit button in on our conversation!

■

Knock-knock.
Who's there?
Creeper.
How are you knocking on the door?

■

Knock-knock.
Who's there?
Slime.
Slime who?
Slime you let me in.

■

Knock-knock.
Who's there?
Stan.
Stan who?
Stan back, I'm gonna blow this door down!

■

Knock-knock.
Who's there?
Juicy.
Juicy who?
Juicy any hostile mobs nearby?

■

## KNOCK-KNOCK. YOU SCARED?

Knock-knock.
Who's there?
Wither.
Wither who?
Wither or without her, get out here and help me look for iron ore!

■

Knock-knock.
Who's there?
Ice cream.
Ice cream who?
Ice cream every time I see a creeper!

# CHATPER 8
## IT'S GHASTLY!

Q: **How do you feel if you see a floating mob overhead?**
A: A-ghast!

■

Q: **What's a ghast's favorite dance?**
A: The Boogie-Woogie.

■

Q: **How do ghasts open doors?**
A: With spook-keys.

**Q: How do ghasts hear so well?**

A: Because they're so ear-ie.

**Q: Why should you run from a fireball?**

A: Because they're ghastly.

■

**Q: Why should you give ghasts a break?**

A: They're just trying to *eek* out a living.

**Q: How do ghasts fly long distances?**
A: They take a scareplane.

**Q: Why do ghasts shoot fireballs?**
A: If they shot water, they'd evaporate.

**Q: Why didn't the ghast ever do its chores?**
A: It Nether had the time.

**Q: What happened between Steve and the Nether portal?**
A: It left him a-ghast.

■

**Q: When do ghasts get most of their work done?**
A: They work from Moan-Day to Fright-Day.

■

**Q: What do ghasts drink?**
A: Le-moan-ade.

Q: **What does a ghast wear when it wants to look fancy?**
A: A boo tie.

Q: **Where do little ghasts go when their parents are at work?**
A: Dayscare.

**Q: Why was the Nether resident freaked out by a fisherman?**

A: Because it was a-ghast.

■

**Q: Why are ghasts bad liars?**

A: Because you can see right through them.

■

**Q: Why are ghasts so lonely?**

A: Because they ain't got no body.

Q: What's in a ghast's nose?
A: Boo-gers.

Q: What do you call adult ghasts?
A: Groan-ups.

Q: What do ghasts wear on their feet?
A: Boo-ts.

**Q: Why do ghasts go to football games?**
A: To boo the referees.

■

**Q: What's a ghast's favorite kind of music?**
A: The boos.

■

**Q: How do ghasts keep up their strength?**
A: They eat plenty of spook-ghetti.

Q: **What do you call ghasts that watch other ghasts work?**

A: Spook-tators.

■

Q: **What's the difference between a creeper and a ghast?**

A: One is a blast and the other is . . . a ghast.

■

Q: **What position would a ghast play in soccer?**

A: Ghoul-tender.

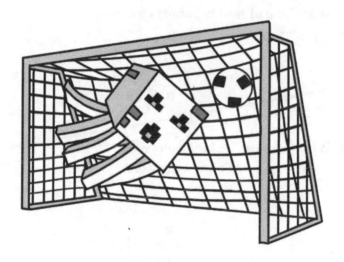

**Q: Why do ghasts make great cheerleaders?**

A: Because they've got spirit.

■

**Q: What do ghasts put on bagels?**

A: Scream cheese.

**Q: What kind of hostile haunts chickens?**
A: A poultry-ghast.

■

**Q: Why do ghasts make spooky noises?**
A: Because they don't know the words.

■

**Q: Why did the ghast get a makeover?**
A: To feel boo-tiful.

■

**Q: What does a ghast wear to see better?**
A: Spook-tacles.

**Q: Why did the ghast have to wear those spectacles?**
A: It was short-frighted.

■

**Q: How do you get a ghast out of your house?**
A: With scare freshener.

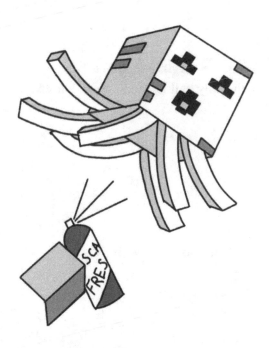

Q: **How do you calm down an angry fireball-shooting ghast?**

A: Throw some water at him and he'll blow off some steam.

■

Q: **Why are ghasts terrible at sports?**

A: Because the only ball they can use is a fireball.

■

Q: **What's a good name for a ghast?**

A: Mona.

**Q: Why couldn't the ghast go out and bug Steve?**
A: It forgot to renew its haunting license.

■

**Q: What kind of ghasts can get to you even if you're in an incredibly tall tower?**
A: One with high spirits.

# CHAPTER 9
## LIMERICKS

There was a Minecrafter named Mick,
Who was quite incredibly thick.
He came upon some gravel,
Mick said, "This should be no hassle."
And took out his new diamond pick.

■

There was a Minecrafter named Dave
Who thought himself to be very brave.
He said "I'm not a clown,
I'll just dig straight down!"
And that's the last time we saw Dave.

■

I just built a house with a floor
With windows, and thick iron door.
There's just one small hitch:
I didn't include a switch.
Now I can't go outside anymore.

■

I woke up this morning in sand
As the sun rose up over the land.
As quick as could be,
I punched down a tree
With only my invincible hand!

■

There was a Minecrafter named Bobby
Who'd developed a sinister hobby.
He would knock on a door,
Put his pick to the floor,
And with TNT make a new lobby.

■

There once was a player named Steve,
Who went out to mine in the eve.
We didn't quite know it,
Creeper would try to blow it,
All up before he could leave.

■

As he mined deeper
He continued to go steeper.
Then he got very brave,
Ventured into a cave
And he came face to face with a creeper!

■

There once was a man named Steve
Who was known for being quite naïve.
So he dug straight down,
And soon had a frown,
As swimming in lava was all he could achieve.

■

As all players probably know,
All diamonds are located below.
For level eighteen
Is where I have been,
And I've got the diamonds to show!

■

A lava moat built to protect us all?
The best idea ever, and also my call.
But I made a goof,
And I fell from the roof.
Oh, why did I make the sides so tall?

■

Myself, I was never a leaper,
But the other direction looked steeper.
So I gave it a go,
And what do you know,
I landed on top of a...*sssssssss*

■

The witch has a giant nose
I wonder just how long it goes?
She is a true potion master
And causes a big disaster.
But I still I wonder about that nose.

■

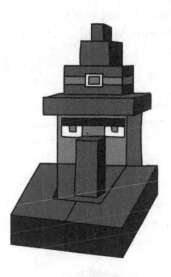

The bow, the bow,
You hold it quite low,
You use it to snipe,
You hold it tight,
It's, of course, much more useful than a hoe!

■

Once you have acquired some reeds
Be careful to plant them like seeds.
But don't use them too fast,
Or they'll be your last.
And just won't fulfill all your needs.

■

When mining deep underground,
Be careful: always hide what you've found.
For unless you do so,
Your treasures shall go,
For here, the Endermen do abound!

If you find yourself facing a Wither,
Take absolute care not to dither.
Ready your sword,
Be strong as a horde,
And upon your foe strike a big fissure!

After mining a lot of diamond ore
I took a nice walk on the shore.
Then a creeper came by,
And blew me up sky high.
And then my diamonds were no more!

■

In the cavernous labyrinths of stone
Mobs in the darkness, they moan.
But ready that pick
And have torches to stick
And make all those treasures your own!

# CHAPTER 10

## MINECRAFT NIGHT AT THE MOVIES

*Attack the Block*

■

*How to Train Your Ender Dragon*

*Zombie Pigmen in Black*

■

*Scott Pigman vs. the World*

■

*Zombee Movie*

■

*Alice in Netherland*

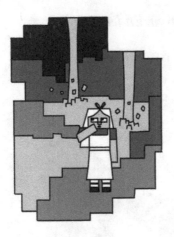

*Iron Golem Man*

*Monster Egg University*

■

*Nether Say Nether Again*

■

*Ghastbusters*

■

*Ender Dragon's Game*

■

*The Blaze Runner*

■

*Star Ores*

■

*Endermen in Black*

# MINECRAFT NIGHT AT THE MOVIES

*The Nether-Ending Story*

■

*Spider Jockey-Man*

■

*The Search for Block*

■

*Strange Brew*

■

*The Hunger Games*

*Creeping with the Enemy*

■

*Blocky*

■

*Blocky II*

■

*Blocky III*

■

*Blocky IV*

*Blocky V*

■

*Gleaming the Cube*

■

*Here Comes the Boom*

■

*Joe Dirt*

■

*Diamonds are Forever*

*Howl's Floating Castle*

■

*Swamp Biome Thing*

■

*Ice Plains Drifter*

■

*Finding D-orey*

■

*The Dark Night*

# MINECRAFT NIGHT AT THE MOVIES

*Journey to the Center of the Earth*

■

*John Carter*

■

*Jeepers Creepers*

■

*The Hurt Blocker*

■

*A Beautiful Mine*

*Mine-ions*

■

*Megamine*

■

*Mine-ore-ity Report*

■

*Zoocreeper*

■

*My Sister's Creeper*

*The Ghast House on the Left*

■

*Ghast Rider*

■

*Zombieland*

■

*Pigman on Campus*

■

*Enderman's Game*

*Crafter Earth*

■

*Happily Ever Crafter*

■

*Blast Man Standing*

■

*Pete's Ender Dragon*

■

*Ender Dragon Ball Z*

*Napoleon Dynamite*

■

*The Flint-Stones*

■

*In Like Flint*

■

*Man of Steel*

■

*Blazing Saddles*

*Elder Guardians of the Galaxy*

■

*Coal Mountain*

■

*Clan of the Cave Spider*

■

*The Boxtrolls*

■

*Now You Seed Me*

# CHAPTER 10

## EXTRAS

## MINECRAFT FOR EVERYONE!

If you were a pickle, you'd play Brinecraft.

If you were a French performer who didn't speak, you'd play Mimecraft.

If you were a poet, you'd play Rhymecraft.

If you were no longer eight and weren't quite ten, you'd play Ninecraft.

If you were Tarzan, you'd play Vinecraft.

If you made short videos on Twitter, you'd play Vinecraft.

If you wanted to play just an okay game, you'd play Finecraft.

If you were a tree, you'd play Pinecraft.

If the only item you could use in Minecraft was string, you'd be playing Twinecraft.

If you were a fork, you'd play Tinecraft.

If you were a pig, you'd play Swinecraft.

If you were a dog, you'd play Caninecraft.

If you were a cow, you'd play Bovinecraft.

If you were a cat, you'd play Felinecraft.

If you were a horse, you'd play Equinecraft.

If you were a bear, you'd play Ursinecraft.

If you were always complaining, you'd play Whinecraft.

If you were a grape, you'd play Winecraft.

If you were a red octagon that had STOP written all over you, you'd play Signcraft.

If you were an orange peel, you'd play Rindcraft.

If you were the sun, you'd play Shinecraft.

If you were hungry, you'd play Dinecraft.

If you were a pilot, you'd play Airlinecraft.

If you were a skier, you'd play Alpinecraft.

If you had a backbone, you'd play Spinecraft.

If you were a singer, you'd play Mikecraft.

If you were a battery, you'd play Alkalinecraft.

If you were a video game creator, you'd play Designcraft.

If you were a lab-made monster, you'd play Frankensteincraft.

On New Year's Eve, you'd play Auld Lang Synecraft.

If you were a newspaper reporter, you'd play Headlinecraft.

If you were a teacher, you'd play Assigncraft.

If you were filthy, you'd play Grimecraft.

If you were a bad guy, you'd play Crimecraft.

If you were a doorbell, you'd play Chimecraft.

If you quit playing Minecraft, you'd play Resigncraft.

# FAVORITE BANDS OF MINECRAFTERS

Imagine Ender Dragons

Rolling Stones

Lead Zeppelin

Metallica

Iron Maiden

Tool

Hole

Stone Roses

The Box Tops

The Zombies

The Bangles

Band of Horses

Bloc Party

Teardrop Explodes

Cake

Cat Stevens

The Darkness

Earth, Wind, and Fire

Massive Attack

Rockpile

Stone Temple Pilots

Sugarcubes

The Village People

Ed Shearin'

Roy Orb-ison

Miner Threat

E-mine-m

New Kids on the Block

A Block of Seagulls

Minekraftwerk

# YOU KNOW YOU'RE BAD AT MINECRAFT WHEN . . .

. . . An Enderman won't even look at you.

. . . Villagers throw themselves to the zombies just to get away.

. . . You made a zombie burst into flames at midnight.

. . . Ghasts cry!

. . . Crops wilt when you stand next to them.

. . . You invited a creeper to your house for dinner.

. . . You tried to build a pool in the Nether.

. . . You tried to fight a creeper with a sword.

. . . You tried to mine bedrock with your bare hands.

. . . You ran out of blocks in Creative Mode.

# YOU KNOW YOU'RE A MINECRAFTER WHEN . . .

You have lines of magic dust stretching throughout your house.

You're out in public and embarrass yourself by jumping and screaming when you hear a hissing noise.

You punch trees in public until your fist is bloody.

You think you can dig through solid rock with your bare hands.

You notice you're running low on firewood, so you go outside and punch a few trees.

You built a hundred-foot-tall tower in front of your house to remember where you live.

You carry a bucket of water with you everywhere you go, just in case.

You try to dig through some rocks with a wooden axe.

You try to shove a cubic mile of gravel into your backpack.

You think chickens come from throwing an egg.

You don't want to go out at night because you're afraid of mobs.

You see everything as cubes.

You don't see anything wrong with beating up livestock.

You're surprised when stuff you leave on the ground doesn't instantly get bigger.

You're shocked when you put a few rocks on top of a couple of sticks and expect them to form a pickaxe.

You've gotten into trouble for digging into your bedroom floor.

You dig holes by punching the ground.

You think bacon takes five seconds to cook.

You watch a zombie movie, and when a zombie dies you ask, "Why didn't it drop anything?"

You step on a spider and think about turning it into a bow.

You find a stick and two rocks on the ground and immediately think, "Hey, free sword!"

You try to dye your hair pink with only a rose and a bone.

You're seriously considering putting a lava moat around your house.

You've replaced all the light fixtures in your house with torches.

You think iron is more valuable than gold.

You believe farmers obtain wool by punching sheep until it falls off.

Your neighbors have asked you to stop trying to dig underneath their houses.

You pour out a bucket of water and are surprised when it doesn't keep flowing forever.

You think your leather suit looks pretty good.

You've thought about how much easier it would be to remember people's names if they floated above them wherever they went.

Yard work for you usually ends with a couple of broken fists.

You've got an impressively large collection of dirt and sand.

You don't understand why you don't get a speed boost when your car passes another car.

You see a report about arson on the news and say, "That's some awful grief."

You've tried to swim up a waterfall.

You tried to swim up a waterfall while carrying a few tons of iron ore.

You think any ailment can be cured with bacon or raw meat.

The only piece of furniture in your room is a big treasure chest.

You've made blueprints to build a minecart system underneath your house.

You've planted a protective wall of cacti around your home.

You've traded in your bike or car for a minecart.

You carry diamond-mining tools with you at all times . . . just in case.

Your nicest outfit is a suit of gold armor.

You've tried to smelt ingot in your microwave oven.

You're *really* afraid of spiders.

Your brain can no longer recognize circles and spheres.

The entire world looks pixelated and in low-resolution.

You go to the beach and say, "Look at all this sandstone!"

You order your steaks raw.

Every time you look at that skeleton in science class, you guard your knees.

Chickens make you nervous.

You're pretty sure you were born on sand.

Your kneejerk reaction is to scream and run away when somebody opens a can of soda.

You press the "T" button on a keyboard whenever you need to talk in real life.

You listen to your favorite song by putting a diamond in a box.

You try to make your own fireworks on the Fourth of July by putting gunpowder and sand into a box.

You never seem to sit or lie down.

You have no idea what a round cake is.

You hope to one day be wealthy enough to live in a red brick house.

You get bored with your life and try to put a new skin on it every few weeks.

You've tried to make a cake with three buckets of milk and two sugar canes.

Seeing zombies on fire would be no big deal to you.

The first thing you do in the morning is look around for tiny floating arrows.

You've replaced all the electrical outlets in your house with redstone.

You cook all your meals in lava.

You store all your wealth in a treasure chest instead of a bank.

You think there's twenty minutes in a day.

You're pretty sure you could ride a pig.

You've placed your lit-up Halloween Jack o' Lanterns underwater.

All the bowls in your house are full of mushrooms.

You've ripped out all the flowers in your yard and tried to dye your dog's fur.

You've fished in a swimming pool.

You've fished in your bathroom.

You want to name your kids "Clay" and "Stone."

You've arranged all of your school supplies into groups of sixty-four.

You write your homework in eight-bit characters.

You've tried to make your own glass by putting a bunch of sand in your oven.

You wish your watch could tell you when it's dawn and dusk.

The hardware store is tired of you asking where they keep the ingots.

You've drawn durability bars on all of your yard tools.

You've wished your arms were rectangular.

When you get really hungry, you wish you could switch to Peaceful Mode so you won't get any hungrier.

You don't like to let your pets out in the yard because you're afraid a zombie might get them.

You just see a fireplace as one big fire hazard.

Your favorite chore is dusting.

You don't like ironing because it doesn't involve any smelting.

You sleep with the lights on, because that way no creepers can spawn in your bedroom.

There are sixty-four items in your backpack right now.

You won't dig in your backyard out of fear of striking lava.

You go to bed the moment the sun sets.

You know exactly how much water is in a swimming pool: about two buckets' worth.

When the power goes out, you say "time to make a new redstone circuit."

You get disappointed when you go into a craft store and it's just a bunch of scrapbooking stuff instead of pickaxes and swords.

You know world peace could be achieved if everybody just went on peaceful mode.

When someone says "jump," you hit the space bar.

You have strong opinions one way or the other about Herobrine.

# MINECRAFT TONGUE TWISTERS

Ghostly ghasts gather gleefully to golf on ghostly golf courses.

If two witches would watch two watches, which witch would watch which watch?

Which witch wished which wicked wish?

Several spooky slimes slam Steve's spawn slightly.

Seven spindly spiders spin spooky silk speedily.

The last ghast to pass has to fast.

Crazy creepers keep creepily killing 'crafts!

The weather in the Nether never wavers.

Purpur pillars.

Steve snacks softly on bacon on a beacon.

# MINECRAFT ANAGRAMS

MINECRAFT = Me? Frantic!

MINECRAFT= Fat mincer

MINECRAFT = Manic fret

BIOMES = Zombies (+Z!)

POTION = Option

HOSTILE MOB = I bolt homes

ENDER MAN = Mannered

# MINECRAFT PROVERBS

A golden apple a day keeps the golden doctor away.

Rome wasn't built in a day and neither was your house.

Make it . . . or break it.

Whoever smelt it dealt it.

If at first you don't succeed, spawn spawn again.

Sticks and stones can break my bones, but you can do a whole lot of other things with them, too.

The only things certain are death and axes.

If you build it, they will come.

Home is where the heart, heart, heart, heart, heart, heart, heart, heart, heart, heart is.

Measure twice, build once, then undo it, and then do it again.

# REAL WORLD JOBS FOR MINECRAFTERS

- Bricklayer

- Construction. *Any* construction.

- Box office manager

- Door-to-door salesman

- Demolitions expert

- Bomb diffuser

- Gravedigger

- Box mover

- Ditch-digger

- Barn raiser

- Architect